FIERCE FISH

by Mignonne Gunasekara
& Charis Mather

Minneapolis, Minnesota

Credits

Images are courtesy of Shutterstock.com. With thanks to Getty Images, Thinkstock Photo, and iStockphoto.
RECURRING – Amovitania. COVER – braingraph. 4–5 – Alessandro De Maddalena, DegrooteStock. 6–7 – Ramon Carretero, Sergey Uryadnikov. 8–9 – Rich Carey, Aquabluedreams. 10–11 – kudla, Oleksandr (Alex) Zakletsky, CC BY 4.0, via Wikimedia Commons. 12–13 – MikhailSh, Rich Carey. 14–15 – Athapet Piruksa, FormosanFish. 16–17 – Hayati Kayhan, guentermanaus. 18–19 – blue-sea.cz, Andriy Nekrasov. 20–21 – Francesco_ Ricciardi, Sascha Janson. 22–23 – Martin Prochazkacz, Altrendo Images. 24 – Hayati Kayhan.

Bearport Publishing Company Product Development Team

President: Jen Jenson; Director of Product Development: Spencer Brinker; Managing Editor: Allison Juda; Associate Editor: Naomi Reich; Associate Editor: Tiana Tran; Art Director: Colin O'Dea; Designer: Elena Klinkner; Designer: Kayla Eggert; Product Development Assistant: Owen Hamlin

Library of Congress Cataloging-in-Publication Data is available at www.loc.gov or upon request from the publisher.

ISBN: 979-8-88916-574-3 (hardcover)
ISBN: 979-8-88916-579-8 (paperback)
ISBN: 979-8-88916-583-5 (ebook)

© 2024 BookLife Publishing
This edition is published by arrangement with BookLife Publishing.

North American adaptations © 2024 Bearport Publishing Company. All rights reserved. No part of this publication may be reproduced in whole or in part, stored in any retrieval system, or transmitted in any form or by any means, electronic, mechanical, photocopying, recording, or otherwise, without written permission from the publisher.

For more information, write to Bearport Publishing, 5357 Penn Avenue South, Minneapolis, MN 55419.

CONTENTS

Welcome to the World of Predators.. 4
Mighty Great White Sharks 6
Brutal Great Barracudas 8
Extreme Electric Eels...............10
Ruthless Red Lionfish...............12
Strange Blotched Snakeheads.......14
Painful Red-Bellied Piranhas........16
Scary Reef Stonefish............... 18
Sneaky Striped Anglerfish......... 20
Fierce and Frightening.............22
Glossary..........................24
Index............................24

WELCOME TO THE WORLD OF PREDATORS

Predators are everywhere in the animal world. These animals hunt other animals for food.

Some fish are powerful predators. Their **prey** does not stand a chance!

Get ready to meet **fierce** fish.

MIGHTY Great White SHARKS

Great white sharks are the biggest predator fish in the world. They can be around 20 feet (6 m) long.

These sharks use their strong sense of smell to hunt.

They bite into their prey with hundreds of sharp teeth.

7

Brutal Great BARRACUDAS

At more than 5 ft (2 m) long, great barracudas are a scary sight.

They have a long lower jaw that sticks out.

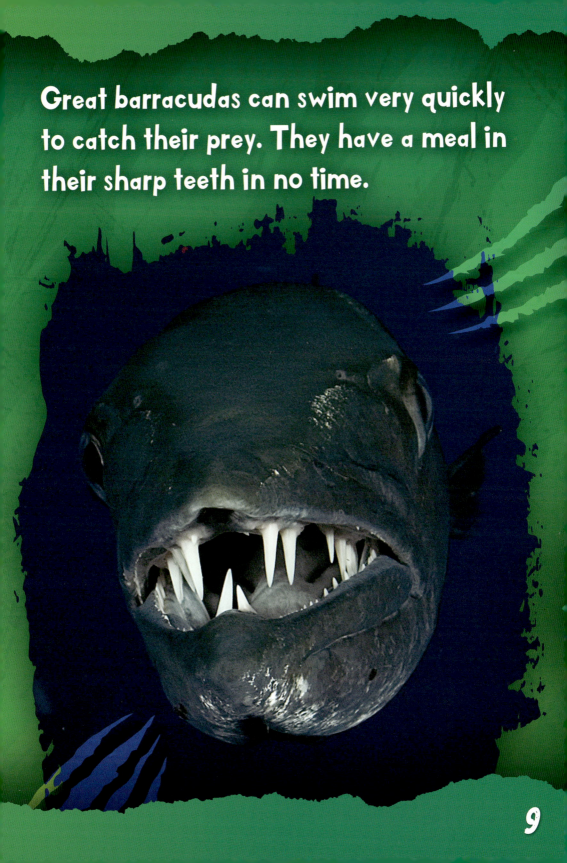

Great barracudas can swim very quickly to catch their prey. They have a meal in their sharp teeth in no time.

EXTREME ELECTRIC EELS

Electric eels can make **electricity** in their bodies. *Zap!* They use it to **stun** their prey.

Many animals know not to mess with these eels.

Their electric shocks are strong enough to hurt even larger animals.

RUTHLESS RED LIONFISH

Red lionfish have **venomous** spines. These points coming from their fins can give a very painful sting.

Spines

Sometimes, the fish corner prey with their fins.

Other times, they wait for their prey to come close. Then the red lionfish swallow them whole. *Gulp!*

STRANGE Blotched SNAKEHEADS

Unlike most fish, blotched snakeheads can breathe out of water.

However, they still do their eating below the waves.

Blotched snakeheads wait for small fish to come near. Then, they attack.

PAINFUL Red-Bellied PIRANHAS

Red-bellied piranhas are scavengers.

This means they will eat dead plants and animals.

But red-bellied piranhas hunt live prey, too.

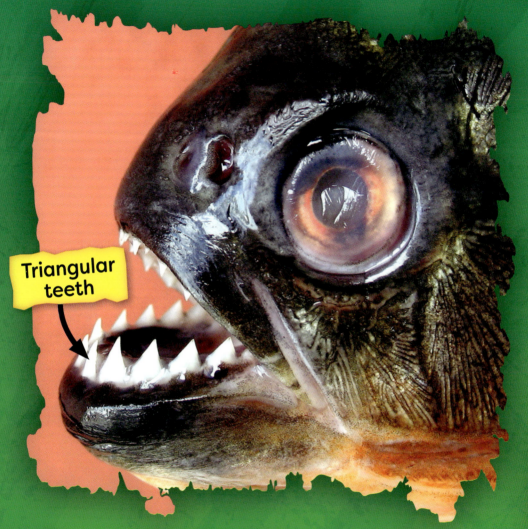

Triangular teeth

They use their good hearing to find prey. Then, they rip apart the meal with their sharp, triangular teeth.

Scary Reef STONEFISH

Reef stonefish can **camouflage** themselves against the sea floor.

These fierce predators sit very still and wait for their prey to come near.

Once a meal is within reach, the stonefish sucks in its food.

SNEAKY STRIPED ANGLERFISH

The striped anglerfish hides in plain sight, too.

Lure

But this predator also has a worm-shaped growth on its head. This is called a lure.

The anglerfish sits still and wiggles its lure. As curious prey come closer to see it, the fish quickly sucks them up.

FIERCE AND FRIGHTENING

Fish come in many shapes and sizes. They each have their own special ways to hunt.

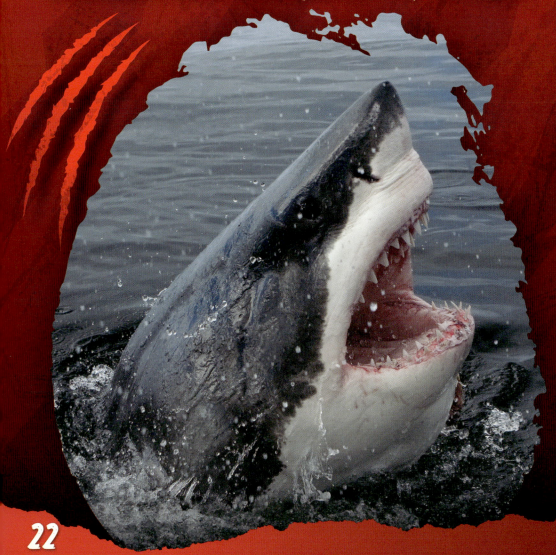

Some have sharp teeth or electric bodies. Others can suck up their prey whole.

They are all fierce in their own way!

Glossary

camouflage to hide by blending in with the surroundings

electricity a type of energy that can cause a painful shock

fierce very dangerous and violent

prey animals that are hunted for food

stun to shock something so that it is unable to move

venomous poisonous to another animal through a bite or sting

Index

electricity 10
fins 12
hunt 4, 7, 17, 22
lure 20–21
prey 5, 7, 9–10, 12–13, 17–18, 21, 23

spine 12
teeth 7, 9, 17, 23
venomous 12

24